An Undiscussed Reality

OCTAVIA MARIE

authorHOUSE®

AuthorHouse™
1663 Liberty Drive
Bloomington, IN 47403
www.authorhouse.com
Phone: 833-262-8899

Published by AuthorHouse 08/09/2021

ISBN: 978-1-6655-3423-9 (sc)
ISBN: 978-1-6655-3422-2 (e)

Print information available on the last page.

This book is printed on acid-free paper.

Contents

Introduction

For as long as I can remember I have always wanted to write a book. But how do I start, what do I write about? There were all kinds of questions that filled my mind which actually prevented me from getting started. I know that I have so much value to give but I lacked the guidance and know how. But here I am today. After reading several self-development books, I have finally decided that this book isn't going to get written unless I actually sit down and do it. I needed to stop worrying about how it's going to get done, just have faith that it needs to be written and to sit down and do it. So here I am. Writing my first book. I hope that you find as much value in my journey as I have. These life lessons have shaped me into who I am today and I am grateful for my experiences because if I didn't have them then I would be a completely different person and this would be a completely different book. My goal is to help as many people as I can overcome struggles, find healing, and find their inner beauty and worth as I have done for myself.

This book was created because there is a harsh stigma surrounding pregnancy termination and as a result it often goes undiscussed. There are so many people who are faced with this undiscussed reality and who are suffering alone during these traumatic events. This book is meant to shed light on what an experience like this is like and to help support others through their own experience and know that they are not alone.

CHAPTER 1

The Life Altering Decision

It was the hardest decision I have ever had to make in my life. My mind and soul felt as if it was filled with complete darkness and this went on for no less than a month. Darkness to the point that all I can really even remember is well, just that, darkness. I could not pull myself out of bed for the life of me. I could barely meet my most basic needs. The only time I could gather enough energy was to use the washroom. I barely even had enough will to eat most of the time. My children had witnessed their typically happy and outgoing mother, fall into full out depression. Depression like I have never felt in my life. I say depression because it is the only thing that I can relate the experience to, having never felt it before. I didn't know for sure though if it was depression I was experiencing. Perhaps it was a mixture of grief and stress that, this decision that I needed to make, was placing on me. Whatever it was, it just felt like too much to bear and they were feelings and emotions that I had never experienced before in my life.

It was during this dark time that I had come to the decision that I needed to make. My time was up. It was now, or deal with the consequences that would follow if I didn't. Before making any moves I needed answers, I needed guidance and most of all I needed support. I needed to hear both sides of the stories. I had discussed both sides of the stories with people who had opposing views and beliefs. And this helped me through the process of making this life altering decision.

I know that there are so many others out there who may or may not have the kind of support I talk about in this book. And I also know that there are so many others who, or whatever reason, won't talk about this at all regardless if they have the support or not. There is so much stigma and judgment around this topic that so many people might just be scared to discuss this, and understandably so. And well, I am here today to shed some light on my experience in hopes that it will help others. Those who want to talk about it, and those who don't. And help them to come to a decision that best suits their needs.

This decision not only altered my life and who I am as an individual. It altered the life of my children and each person who was important in our lives at the time. It was a decision that did not only affect me but others around me as well, and that much I was fully aware of. Although I was considerate of everyone else around me, it was still my decision, and my decision alone to make. Perhaps this is why this decision was so hard to make, though. Maybe it was the reason why it took me several weeks to make. It was by far, the biggest decision I have ever had to make in my entire life. And big decisions like this shouldn't be taken lightly. It shouldn't be easy. And a decision like this, absolutely came with pain. The pain that I felt was my mind and body's way of telling how important this decision really was. The pain was indescribably strong. Pain so crippling that all I could see at the time was darkness. Not all pain is physical, but it may have been hard to tell at the time that it wasn't physical pain but spiritual.

CHAPTER 2

The Pill

I did it. I pushed through the pain and the fear and I made my final decision. I was 8 weeks and 6 days along. I had waited until the absolute last day that it was safe to terminate this pregnancy by consuming the pill, this is called a medical termination. Otherwise I would have to pursue other options, such as a surgical termination, which is much more invading and possibly much more heart wrenching. And I knew that I wouldn't be able to go the surgical route because I personally felt like it could have been much more traumatizing than what I was already going through. So I had to make my decision now because the time to do so had run out. And so that's what I did, the day had come. I saw the doctor who requested an urgent ultrasound to see exactly how far along I was to ensure I wasn't too far along or the pill. The ultrasound technician warned me that they typically do not show the ultrasound screen to the bearer as it may be too painful. But I requested to look because I needed to be aware of what I was doing. I needed to know that I was making the right decision for me. And for myself I guess it was a way of showing my respects. After all, this was a part of myself no matter how it's looked at.

And then I was straight off to the doctor who wrote out my prescription. I headed straight to the pharmacy and I picked up my prescription. Once I had the prescription, I held that pill in my hand for at least an hour. I knew this was it. There is no turning back once I swallow this pill. This was the hardest pill I would ever have to swallow.

I hesitated. I hesitated even though I had consciously made the decision to follow through. Every muscle in my body was tense. My body was shaking. Every thought that I had previously thought of, in regards to terminating or not, had once again run through my mind. Questioning once again if this was the right decision for me to make. I just had to be absolutely one hundred percent sure that I was making the decision that was for me.

I had a friend with me on this day to help me follow through with my decision because I was clear about what I wanted and I needed that support to ensure that I did, in fact, follow through. I needed that support and was grateful to have someone by my side strong enough to help me carry the weight on this day. Someone who was impartial so that their emotions didn't interfere with my decision making and/or make the process harder. I had a couple other friends on my phone, talking with me and supporting me all the way through. Friends from both sides, Friends who wished I would not terminate, and others who believed it was in my best interest at the time. This kind of support shows true strength in friendship. The fact that we may have had differing beliefs and they were still by my side supporting me. After an hour of holding on to that pill in hesitation, I finally swallowed it.

The doctors have informed me that medical termination is not safe after the 9 week period which is when the embryo is forming into a fetus. So at 8 weeks 6 days pregnant, I had no choice. This was the last day it was safe to terminate the pregnancy by pill form.

As previously stated, this wasn't easy to do, by any means. I was so scared. Scared that it wouldn't work properly and put my health at risk, scared that it wouldn't work properly and I would have to terminate through alternative measures. But most of all I was scared that I was making a massive mistake. The support that I had during this time made this somewhat bearable and somewhat easier to follow through with. I am not sure what I would have done without the support. I don't know if I would have been able to swallow that pill. I felt nauseous, guilt, unease, and unsure. I had this pit in my stomach that I could not shake. These were feelings and emotions that I never want to revisit as long as I live. However, I am grateful for all the support that I did have because I don't know how I would have coped otherwise or if I would have been able to come to the decision that I did. Even if I did come to the same decision (which I likely would have), it would have been a much harder experience than it already was.

I know that support may not always be an obvious option, but if you are willing to reach out, there are people who will always be willing to help. It may not be friends or family. But support can be sought out at women's centre's or help lines etc. It may not be as personal. But support is out there. There are so many people out there who truly do care even when it doesn't feel like it. You are not alone.

CHAPTER 3

The Process

This chapter night be too much information for some as potentially gruesome details are described. Just skip ahead to the next chapter if you need to. Reader's discretion is advised.

About four hours after consuming the pill, my body began to bleed. It is so hard to even try to explain the feelings that were happening within me. I did not feel physical pain during the process but I felt scared and I felt sad. And I know that a part of me was even trying to consciously block out what was really happening. I was in complete denial of what was even happening. I didn't want to have to experience it. It's too much for anyone to have to bear. About four or five hours after the bleeding had started, the embryo had passed. I almost felt as if I was in shock. It was hard to believe what was happening or what I had done. What had I done?

In earlier discussions throughout this day, a friend had asked me what I would do with the embryo. At that point I hadn't really thought about it. I was just going to flush it. But the discussion opened up to alternative options, such as burring it under a tree and planting that tree outdoors in the spring so that it would have a respectful place to rest. I thought that was a really great idea, so I figured I would like to try it. After all, this was a life in formation and deserved some kind of respectful place to rest and be remembered by. Right or wrong? That is only for the bearer to decide.

At approximately 9 weeks along, an embryo would be about the size of a bean. Unfortunately, amongst the placenta and other pregnancy related parts, I wasn't actually able to find the embryo in all that had passed. I guess I didn't actually know what I was looking for. So I said my peace and took some photos, as disturbing as that sounds, in case I missed something and would later on be able to point it out. Even though that wouldn't have done me any good anyway. And I also think it was probably better that I didn't know because knowing and having the images in my mind may have been haunting for me to have to remember. But my body and mind was in a bit of a shock so I don't think I was thinking a hundred percent straight, anyways.

I then made my peace and flushed everything down the toilet. I was informed that the bleeding should slow down quite a bit once everything had passed but it stayed heavy for at least 24 more hours. That began to concern me. I then learned the next day that it was because not everything had passed. More pregnancy related parts had passed, even though I don't know what exactly it was. That's when the bleeding had slowed down almost completely. It was basically just spotting from there on out for a couple of days.

CHAPTER 4

Aftershock

Part of me wanted to believe that the little life in the making was still inside me. I would still hold my lower belly as if it were. I know that it took a while for my mind and body to learn what had actually happened because I felt pregnancy symptoms for several months after the termination. I continued to have heartburn for about two months post termination and my hormones were all over the place for about the same amount of time. I spent countless hours overcoming the depression symptoms. I cried more than I thought I was ever capable of. I was unhappy, sad, and also still very much in denial.

However, I knew that I had no choice but to come to terms with the decision that I had made. And I had to take advantage of all the support that I had and work my way through this. Keeping in mind that the entire month, prior to consuming the pill, I was in a state of darkness as I discussed in a previous chapter. Well, The day after the termination, I still felt awful but it felt like a huge weight had been lifted off my shoulders. Not in the sense that I was happy about it, more like I was just so relieved that I no longer had to fret over making this huge decision. It was a done deal.

Day by day, I began to get my energy back. It was a slow process, but I began to recognize myself again and my children were getting their mother back. However, the journey didn't end there. My mind and body had been subjected to so much stress, and that required recovery. For months post termination, I was very moody and I cried all the time, and I am not usually one to cry. I have been the master at bottling up or blocking out emotions. But with this kind of stress, I just couldn't help it. It just become too much to bear and the emotions were just overflowing right out of me. I couldn't even recognize myself.

And I knew, because of prior education and awareness that I couldn't bottle these feelings up because they would find a way to come out whether they come out by expressing emotions, or present themselves in a form of physical ailment. I am not keen on having a physical ailment. After all I have two kids that need their mother to be healthy. And because I also need to be a positive role model and show them that expressing emotions is normal and healthy, so long as these emotions are expressed in a healthy way.

At first, I kept to myself mostly and I looked only to my good friends for support when I needed it, or was comfortable enough to seek and accept it. But it didn't really seem to be enough because there was no one in my inner circle that had experienced what I had, even though every experience differs from person to person. Even with the support I had, I felt very alone.

There was a similar situation, such as a miscarriage, but I still believe that it is not quite the same because a miscarriage is involuntary and doesn't require having to make such a decision. I am not saying that a miscarriage is any less painful, all I am saying is that I just feel like the circumstances are somewhat different and the mental toll it has on a person would differ between the circumstances. I just don't believe that, unless a person has personally terminated a pregnancy voluntarily would understand, just as I couldn't imagine what someone who endured a miscarriage could possibly have experienced. One of these situations is not greater or less than the other, they are just different. With that being said, I honestly appreciated others sharing their experiences with me because in a sense it did make me feel as though I wasn't alone and there are others who care about me enough to share their story with me in attempts to help guide me through my own pain. For that, I am grateful.

CHAPTER 5

When I Found Out

I found out that I was pregnant very early on. My body had given me signs right away. I knew what my body was telling me because I had two pregnancies prior to this one which led to me having two happy and healthy sons. They were aged eight and two at this time. The weekend, however, that I found out that I was pregnant, I was actually on a road trip away from my home town to celebrate my best friend's birthday. We were going to hit up the night clubs and just let go, embrace our youth and have a fun and unforgettable weekend! And an unforgettable weekend it was. Just not the way that we had imagined.

It was about an 8 hour drive to the city where we were going to party and have fun. It was a long trip because we live in a small town and we wanted to experience more. And also because one of our friends lived there too so that was super convenient. I never suspected a thing on the trip down. I thought it was a little odd that I was really tired towards the end of the trip, but I figured it was just from travelling. It wasn't until hindsight that I clued in. Once we arrived in the city, we went out and gathered our drinks for the night. We like to pre-drink to get the party started before actually heading to the club. I found it really hard to drink that night. One drink in and I wasn't feeling very good. My body just felt weird, almost like it was rejecting the alcohol. I felt lightheaded and my body felt tingly.

Well, I finished that one drink and mixed myself another. The second drink, however, I just couldn't drink. I would take little sips here and pretend to drink a little more there because we went out to have fun. And that is what I was trying to accomplish despite how my body was feeling. A few sips in, I just gave up and gave my drink away. I knew my friends probably wouldn't understand but I just couldn't drink it. We had made our way down town and we, as in my friends, because I wasn't feeling well, were ready to hit up the nightclub.

As we were walking to the club, I began to get heart burn, and it was to the point that it was very uncomfortable. I had suggested that we stop at a restaurant on the way because I thought that having a bite to eat would make me feel better. And yeah it did. As we were standing in the restaurant I explained that it is just so odd that I have heartburn because I have only ever gotten heart burn when I was pregnant. And just as that was coming out of my mouth I had a moment of subtle shock. But then my mind corrected me, "Nah, can't be. It must have just been from the drink I had earlier". After we ate, we continued on with our night. Needless to say, I followed my friends around and pretended to have a good time, because after all, it was my best friends birthday weekend and I didn't want to be the party pooper who ruined it for everyone. And that is exactly how I was feeling. Nauseous, light headed, tingly, and like a party pooper. Needless to say, I did not enjoy myself at all and I just wanted to go home and go to bed. This was odd because I always have a blast when we go out, but this time, I couldn't wait for this night to be over.

The next morning, I just couldn't shake that I was feeling that dang heartburn. So, before everyone woke up, I walked to the grocery store. It was a warm and sunny summer day. I can remember the warmth of the sun shining down on me, early in the morning. I can still feel the fresh air and the warm breeze as I walked. It was absolutely gorgeous. I absolutely love warm summer mornings. There is something just so peaceful about it. When I got to town I grabbed some breakfast, and picked myself up a pregnancy test. I was sure that it was going to be negative. But I wanted to go out and party this weekend, and I knew I couldn't do that, in good conscience, if I suspected that I was pregnant. So, I just needed to ease my mind and see that negative test result.

Once I got back to my friend's house, I patiently waited for both of them to wake up. In reality, I think I was just scared to take the test and see what it said. I know that if it was negative, I could move on and enjoy my weekend. But if it said positive, what would that mean for me? My entire life would be altered. That's not such a bad thing. It would just be a different reality than what I was used to. I already have two sons with one man. If I was pregnant, I would have another child with a different man. I couldn't help but wonder how that would change my life. I didn't spend too much time thinking about it because I was sure it was going to be negative anyway. When my friends were both awake I decided to take the test. It felt like forever waiting for the test results. And what seemed like a lifetime later, I checked the stick and there it was, it hit me like a ton of bricks. It said positive. I told myself, and my friends, that it must be wrong because it's just a cheap test, "I should have gotten the good brand!" My friend then mentioned that she had an unused test, but that it was expired so it might not give proper results. This tests' results, too, came back positive. Despite the tests being the cheap brand and the other expired, I finally believed what they said because my body was also telling me the same thing.

There were so many feelings that came over me. Even though it was unexpected, and I had no idea prior as to how this would make me feel, I was actually pretty happy and excited about this. Well, you know, after the shock had settled a bit. I had finally met a man I could see myself creating a family with and that dream was becoming a reality. We were going to be a nuclear family. The first thing I wanted to do was call him and tell him about the news. After all, this is something that we have previously talked about trying for in the future. I mean, we didn't want it to happen so soon, or expect it to, but it did.

So the first thing I did, after I chatted with my friends about it for a bit, was call him. I was excited to tell him the big news. This is basically how the phone call went. I told him the news and this was his reaction, "how could you be pregnant? We will talk about this when you get home". Maybe he was in shock himself. I will never know what went on in his mind but that was not the reaction I ever would have expected. My heart sank right into my stomach because I realized instantly that he certainly didn't feel the same way that I did. And as I later learned, which I will discuss later in this book, that there was a lot that I didn't know about him and how he truly felt.

Let's just say that the rest of the weekend didn't go as planned, at all! Not only did I have my own set of new circumstances. My friend was dealing with her own personal circumstances as well. Something big had happened in her life that had left her in a less than pleasant state. Even though she hid it fairly well. Of course we tried to make her feel better, we all tried to forget about our 'love' lives and just enjoy our weekend together. Easier said than done, but we did our best. Rather than going out to the nightclubs, we did other things such as trying a bunch of different escape rooms. The escape rooms were actually a lot of fun and did help, temporarily, take our minds off of our real life situations. We were debating going to an activity room where you can smash all kinds of stuff like old computers and what not so that we can all let our anger out. But then decided against it and went to the escape rooms instead. I have some pretty awesome friends. They were so kind and supportive and I couldn't have asked for better company during that instantly stressful time. Even though it was my best friend's birthday weekend and we were supposed to party.

CHAPTER 6

Leading up to the Decision

This was by far the hardest decision I have ever had to make. I cannot stress this enough. I don't believe that anyone can really appreciate how incredibly difficult a decision like this is to make unless they have experienced it themselves. My entire life I always thought that I would never be able to terminate a pregnancy because it would go against my nature and that I would somehow be too attached or that I could never dismiss a life or whatever other reason I had for believing this. The thought of terminating this pregnancy had never even crossed my mind once until HE said that he didn't want this pregnancy, this potential child, this life with me and my family. That is when I first thought about the termination and I eventually even began to consider it.

In a sense, maybe he was right. I needed to think about my life, my children's lives, the potential life of the baby if it were to have been brought into this world, and HIS life as well. Most importantly I needed to do what I thought was in everyone's best interest. And that is a lot of weight for anyone to carry.

When HE brought up the thought of termination I had a lot of feelings about it. I was mostly angry and at first completely against the idea. I was in shock that he would even consider it. But I was also really sad and I had a really hard time believing that he would even suggest it. I just felt so rejected and hurt. I guess I could say that I had been in denial about him and the way he really felt about us to begin with. I was so unbelievably naïve. I was sure that there was something so real between us. Well that is what I wanted to believe anyway. However, it turned out that we did not, in fact, share mutual feelings. I had only learned this when I told him that I was pregnant. And for me, this all needed to be considered in the decision making process.

CHAPTER 7

Creating a Lie Together

We have, prior to this experience, talked about having a child together and creating a life together. We definitely did not however, anticipate it to happen so soon, if it could even happen at all. He would always contradict himself by saying that he would like to have kids of his own and that we could start a family together. But then he would say things like he used to have cancer and that he is not able to have kids because of the radiation treatment. And he would also say that he had some tests done and they showed that he wasn't able to have kids. There were so many mixed messages that I didn't know what to believe. If what he said was true about not being able to have kids then I couldn't understand why he would still be making a plan with me to have some together in the future.

Another one of his suggestions, after the initial suggestion to just terminate without thought, was to terminate it and wait and try again in the future. That was not an option I was willing to pursue. In my mind, if he wanted to terminate this pregnancy then we were done. I believe that this is something bigger than both of us and it wasn't something to just mess around with. It was either going to happen or it wasn't. I wasn't going to exchange one life for another just because it was not scheduled to fit his convenience.

CHAPTER 8

Why am I Doing this to Myself?

When I was contemplating this decision, I signed up to an email list that provides updates about the stages of pregnancy development. Every week I would get an email about the growth of the embryo, I watched the videos of the stages of pregnancy and read about what parts of the embryo were developing. This was hard for me because it made it feel so real. And I suppose that was not necessarily a bad thing, because it was very real. As much as I wanted to block out or deny what was happening. The truth was that there was a little life forming inside of me and it was my responsibility to face the reality of it. There was something growing inside of me and it would have been irresponsible of me to pretend like there wasn't no matter how much pain I was in

The other reason I signed up was because I was not set on a decision. I was initially going to keep it, no question. I was taking care of myself and not putting the fetus at any risk of being harmed. I wanted to follow the growth stages just as I did with my children prior. And I think that this is what also made it harder because it was all a complete mind shift from expecting to have this one life where I would have another child and a family, to losing two important things in my life and it being completely different than what I had pictured.

There are so many others that are probably hurting in the same way that I experienced and I believe that I can help many people understand that only they know what is best for themselves. And that only they can make a decision that is in their best interest and that that is okay. I believe that it is important that anyone going through this type of experience knows that they are not alone. You are not alone. Do what you know in your heart is best for YOU.

CHAPTER 9

The Relationship

When I first met him, I felt like it was love at first sight. This is something that never happens to me. Well, it has never happened to me before anyway. I don't know what it was. Maybe it was a familiar feeling about the way he looked. Maybe it was because I was just ready to let my guard down. Maybe it was just a physical attraction that just completely blinded me to everything else. Whatever it was, left me head over heels. We began to see each other regularly and it didn't take long until we were spending every available moment together. I loved every bit of it. We would listen to music and dance together, even though I wasn't the greatest dancer. But we would still have so much fun. We would go on date nights, go to the movies, visit the lake and stay out late with our friends. I met so many of his friends, he met so many of mine. We counted on each other when we needed one other. We were there for each other when the other called. It almost seemed too perfect. It got to the point where we were doing everything together.

And let's not forget about the passion, there was so much energy and passion between us. We couldn't keep our hands off of each other. Like seriously, it was gross. As cheesy as it sounds, even to me because I am so not the type to be all 'lovey dovey', but when he first kissed me I just melted. And again the time after that, and after that. It was like my body was taken over by someone I didn't even recognize.

I was so sure that I had found 'the one'. You know what I mean, the 'one' who we think we would spend the rest of our lives with. I haven't felt passion like I felt for him in a very, very long time. It was as if a part of me that has been sleeping for a decade, had finally been woken up. It didn't take me long to realize that I had fallen deeply in love with him. Maybe it was just puppy love, or lust, I don't really know, but I was under his spell. He would bring me flowers just for the sake of it and I just loved when we cuddled on the couch to watch a movie because he would tell me that we fit so perfect that it was just meant to be. He was just so charming and everything just felt so right and I wouldn't have changed any of it. I guess with great love can come great pain. Who knew?

Well, I think you get the point. This honeymoon phase lasted for a couple months. I thought everything was perfect and I was imagining that this was going to be it and we were creating a life for ourselves together. I was so blinded by this puppy love that I didn't see, or more accurately, I consciously chose to ignore the red flags. Once in a while the universe would throw these red flags my way, trying to warn me, but I chose to ignore them. Like that box of condoms that were in his truck when he went away for the weekend to the rodeo he participated in. Or those condoms that fell out of the dryer when his clothes were taken out. How he refused to allow a photo of the two of us together be posted publicly on social media. I most definitely should have listened to the flag of him smelling like another woman. But when I brought these things up, he would cleverly manipulate his way out of it, and in some circumstances even turn it around on me, claiming that I was in the wrong for making him feel the way that I supposedly did. A lot of the time I just let these things slide to the back of my mind because I was enjoying our relationship so much that I didn't want to believe these things, or allow them to get in the way of us.

I chose to ignore the red flags, and looking back, I think it was because I finally found someone that made me feel so good and I didn't want to give up on that so quick. I am usually always so quick to ditch relationships after a month or two of dating. But I didn't want to ditch this one because I had let my feelings dictate my behaviour rather than use my logical thinking like I normally would have. I didn't want to believe that these red flags meant anything. If that doesn't sound bad enough, he even mentioned a couple times that it sounds like there are red flags…

and I knew where he was going with it but I didn't want to acknowledge it. Why would he be saying this? I didn't want to read between the lines or try to figure out what he meant but I thought was he not as invested into this relationship as I was? Well, as you know, I soon found out the answer to that one.

CHAPTER 10

Who are you?

Remember when I called him and told him that I was pregnant, and his response was "how could you be pregnant?" That man that I had put up so high on the pedestal, the one who I thought was so handsome, charming, kind and thoughtful. He didn't have any kids of his own but he was really great with mine and I thought he would have made an awesome dad. My kids accepted him, and as far as I could tell, he accepted my kids. Well, something shifted in him and in our relationship the moment that I told him I was pregnant. It was as if he turned into a completely different person overnight. Or maybe I was just completely blind to this side of him. I never did give myself the chance to get to know this side of him. Our relationship moved so fast and I only saw what I wanted to see.

While I was still on the road trip with my friends, he at one point over the phone told me that he didn't want this pregnancy. His mind went straight to termination. There was no joy to be seen or heard coming out of him at all. I don't want to speak on his behalf because I don't know what was going on in his mind, but I was left with a pretty sour taste in my mouth. Our relationship went from perfect, happy and fun to miserable and unbearable, literally overnight. It was quite a shocker, to be honest. I had no idea what I had gotten myself into. I like to think of myself as a pretty logical and thought provoking person, but as embarrassing as it is to me, this one just slipped right past me.

When I returned home from the trip, there was nothing but tension between us. I was in complete disbelief about his reaction, and I just wasn't happy about it at all! And he wasn't happy about the pregnancy at all. He made that very clear. He made remarks such as, "you did this on purpose" and "IF that baby is mine". He always dropped these subtle hints that the baby wasn't even his, which also would have meant that he believed that I cheated on him, so he was also accusing me of cheating, which wasn't very nice either.

CHAPTER 11

Reuniting After I Told Him

Okay, to be honest he and I were not getting along very well at all after I told him I was pregnant. I quickly realized that we both had very different reactions and opinions about this pregnancy. I can't speak on his behalf but I believe that he was in shock and not overly happy about this pregnancy. We argued because we had different views on how this should all play out. I just couldn't believe that some of his first thoughts were termination. It was almost as if he hadn't even put any thought into it, he was just set on how he saw his own future playing out and it definitely seemed like I wasn't a part of his vision.

I guess that maybe he felt bad about the things that he had said about the pregnancy and that we were not getting along very well because when I flew home after the weekend away he picked me up from the airport and had brought me some flowers. With the flowers came a little note asking me to 'come home'. I was living at his place more so than I was at my own at the time so he was referring to his place as home. I went home and unpacked and thought about things and took a day away from him to think and then I went to his house the next day to see him and maybe we could come to some sort of agreement about the big elephant in the room.

When I arrived at his place the next day he was working on putting in a fence with his neighbours that he failed to tell me about and he also expected me to help them. He said he needed my help. Of course I wasn't happy about that. I came to his house to see him and to talk about the pregnancy because we really needed to because of the toxicity it was creating between us. Well, I refused to help him build the fence. I think maybe he either forgot that I was pregnant or expected a pregnant woman to help with heavy fence posts. Either way I thought it was super inconsiderate. He was not in a good mood either so I just left his place that day and basically had most of our conversations over the phone from there on out.

CHAPTER 12

The end of the Relationship

Is it obvious enough that this relationship just wasn't going to last? We just couldn't agree on what seemed to be anything anymore. The relationship that I loved, that I was head over heels into, turned into a nightmare nearly over night. We barely talked anymore. Sometimes we would talk a little bit about the future and what that might look like if we went through with the pregnancy. I remember one day we were sitting next to each other on his deck and he made a weird comments like "well you could move in with me but I will probably just leave, but I will leave you with the house." I was like "leave? What do you mean leave, you would just leave us all?" and he would reply with "I don't know". Well, let me tell you that was extremely confusing! I didn't understand what he was talking about. Why would he leave us all I wondered and where was this even coming from. I didn't understand then and I still don't.

Most of our conversations were not very pleasant anymore. A part of me wanted to keep him in my life and in a relationship and keep what we did have alive, but the good parts seemed to be lost and long gone. Because we couldn't seem to agree on anything anymore and were arguing most of the time I decided to move my things out of his house and move back into my own. It took a couple of hours and I did it while he was at work so that we didn't have to argue over that either because at this point I was basically done. I wanted to give our relationship one more shot but it wasn't going to be done by living with him in his house. I didn't want to believe that this was the end of it and I didn't realize it at the time but this was the last time I ever took a step in his house and I only ever saw him once afterwards. And of course that wasn't a pleasant visit either it was just an argument about something stupid. And that was the last time that I ever saw him. I had enough. I was done.

Nothing else seemed to matter anymore. At this point the only thing that mattered was that I was pregnant and alone and I needed to make a decision. The last time I ever talked to him was when I was about 6 weeks pregnant. I called him up and I asked him two very important questions. I needed his answers so that I could make my decision in better conscience knowing that he had his fair say as well. The first question was "do you want this pregnancy?" and his answer was a straight out and firm "no, I do not". The second question I asked was "what would you do if I kept this pregnancy?" he replied with "I would take you to court for sole custody and I will make sure that your other kids are taken away from you too". That was all I needed to hear and I never spoke to him ever again after this day.

CHAPTER 13

Does His Opinion Matter Too?

I know that this is my body and my decision, but I needed to know for sure how he felt about it before I made my final decision. So I asked him straight out if he wanted this baby and he said "no, I do not want this baby". He also said some other hurtful words such as, if I decided to go through with this pregnancy he would take me to court for sole custody of the baby and fight until he got it. And that he would also try to have my two boys taken away from me as well. The fact that someone could even say such things just completely baffled my mind. For starters, there is no way that he would ever win those battles, but that's not the point. The fact that he would even make these threats based off of... what? Wanting to have a relationship with him and keep the baby? I knew that I could not spend any more time on someone like that. I knew for a fact I did not want to bring a child into this world to be fought over for the rest of its life. I strongly believed that we would never have come to an understanding on terminating or not. We would not have agreed on parenting styles, major decisions regarding the potential child such as where they would go to school, how they would have been raised, etc. I felt hopeless and that I was stuck with only one logical decision to make.

CHAPTER 14

Loss and Grief

There is no way at the time that I could really have known if this decision was the right one. In a sense, I don't think that I will ever truly know. It took a really long time to come to terms with all that had happened. But I know it was real. It had to be because that much pain didn't spawn from nothing. Remember when I said that I signed up to get updates about the embryos development? Well, I still got those reminders even a year after the termination. Once a month I open my email and am reminded about how old the baby would now be. Every single time that one of those emails comes in a shock runs through my body and I spend a good portion of the day pondering if I had made the right decision. Most days, I am confident that yes I did make the right decision. I couldn't imagine being tied to that, what I perceive to be a horrible man. But on those days that I receive the updates, I once again questioned everything. The last update that I received, the baby would have been 6 months old. I then imagine what life would be like with a 6 month old baby. I imagine if it would have been a boy or girl and what it would have looked like. These are the days that are the hardest. These are the days that bring back all of the memories and these are the days that I feel the most loss and grief.

I once read an article that said that when a woman is pregnant, whether the baby is brought to term or not, that the baby is connected to the mother on a cellular level. I found this intriguing. No matter what, that little potential life and I are connected forever. I believe that spirits do exist and that we are spirits who dwell inside of our bodies. That spirit had chosen me. And what makes me feel incredibly sad, is that I didn't choose it and the would-be father didn't choose it.

I can come up with any excuse in the book or ways I could have kept it. Yes, there are ways that I could have made it work. I could have picked up our lives, everything that we know and love and moved out of town away from HIM and maybe he would never have found out that I kept it and created a whole new life. Would that have been fair to anyone involved though? To my kids, to the rest of my family to HIM, to myself? Would adoption have been an option? Of course adoption is an option but would any less painful option for myself, my children, or the unborn soul? My family, or his family could have cared for the unborn soul. But in reality, in my reality, these weren't options I was willing to pursue. For the sake of my mental health and all those involved. And when it comes right down to it. The ultimate decision was mine to make and I did what, in my mind, was best for all involved. Unless someone has been in a situation where they are faced to make such a decision, then they have absolutely no right to infringe on another's personal beliefs and opinions.

CHAPTER 15

Right or Wrong

No matter how badly I wanted to block it out I had to face the truth. But with that being said, I kept telling myself that this is no different than taking a morning after pill, or what some call the 'plan B' pill. It was a way to protect myself from believing that what I was doing was wrong. What is right or wrong, though? Is that really for me, or anyone else, to decide? The fact is, is that it just was. Only society decides what is right or wrong and in the case of termination, there is no collective agreement or understanding of whether termination is right or wrong in our society because so many people have different views and beliefs.

From the moment we are born, we are being shaped by our environment and the people around us. Other people's actions and beliefs play a critical role in what we believe is normal and what we believe our reality is supposed to be like. In turn, this shapes our core beliefs and guides our behaviours. And this contributes greatly to the creation of who we become.

My entire life I was raised to believe that terminating a pregnancy was wrong. As I got older, into my adult years, I began to see so many people expressing their opinions on this subject and it was only then when I began to realize that my thoughts about termination were not my own. They were instilled within me by others based off what they believed and because it was said to me over and over again that termination is wrong, I began to believe it without even realizing it. This belief was so engrained into my mind that it just became second nature for me. But when I began to see others' opinions I began to open my mind to other possibilities, other reasoning's, different perspectives, and so on. And I realized that there was no 'one way'. Every single circumstance is different. Every person is different, every person's beliefs are different. Who am I to judge some else's position when I know absolutely nothing about them, their situation, their beliefs, their circumstances? And who is anyone else to judge me?

I did not think that I would ever be the type of person to ever terminate a pregnancy. One, because of the beliefs that were instilled into my mind since I was a child. And two, because the love that I feel for my children is stronger than anything I have ever experienced and I could only imagine that if I became pregnant again that this would also be the case. But sometimes you just don't really know until the time comes and you're actually faced to deal with it and make this kind of decision for yourself. How could anyone truly know until they're faced with it themselves?

That love though, that love is what helped guide me to make this decision. I could not bear the thought of bringing a child into this world who was being fought over since the moment of conception. A father who didn't even seem to take a second to think about termination as a last resort, only a first. A father who seemingly, put no thought into it, immediately demand that a termination was in order. A father who had threatened to dismiss the mother out of the potential baby's life, before it was even born. A father who threatened to take sole custody and guardianship of the potential child, along with threatening to have my two children to be taken away from me. The thought of bringing a child into this toxic environment was gut wrenching. The father could barely take care of himself, how could he possibly take care of a child? He refused to even sit with me and talk about this situation like an adult. His mind, which was expressed through his words and actions, went straight to termination, no question.

As painful as this whole experience was, I honestly believe that it would have been so much more painful for everyone involved if I had not made that decision to terminate. Some of the main things that I needed to consider were, is this child going to be fought over its entire life. Do I even know the father well enough to know if he would even be a suitable person I could trust to leave a child with? It was clear that I did not know him at all despite my previous thoughts and feelings about him. How often would this child see my kids and how would that affect them all? As a mother, I want to eliminate as much trauma in my kids' lives as much as possible and I honestly believed that this child would have been raised in a traumatic and possibly toxic environment. I believe that more harm would have been done than good. It is not fair to a child to bring it into that kind of world.

Did I love that potential life? Of course I did and it was that love and the love that I have for my children and myself that helped guide me to make the decision that I did. I honestly believe that I did what was in the best interest of everyone involved. And that's my story.

CHAPTER 16

Judgement

Love is in the absence of judgement – Dali Lama

You know what was hard? Well besides the WHOLE EXPERIENCE, was driving past the hospital some days when the pro-lifers were standing out there with their picket signs, when I would scroll social media pages and come across the pro-lifers posts. Some would say things like "Don't terminate, we will adopt" or "Did the baby get a choice". These used to make me really upset when I came across things like this but the reality is that these are someone else's beliefs that they are trying to instill into others. How is their belief any more right or wrong than mine? Do these people know what it is like to experience something like this? Probably not. Do they have any idea how traumatic the experience is for the bearer? I really doubt that too. Because if these people with their beliefs and opinions about pro-life knew anything about experiencing this and all the mental strain and heart ache that comes with it. Then in good conscious, they wouldn't be out there attempting to push their judgement and beliefs onto others. Instead, I think that they would be supportive of the person who has experienced such a traumatic event and show kindness and consideration. So in all honesty, those opinions mean nothing. For anyone going through this type of experience, no matter how hard it is, it is important to shrug off the opinions and belies o others and just do what you feel in your own heart is best for you.

I really hope this won't be the case but I know that I may receive a lot of backlash for writing, publishing, and sharing my story. I may receive a lot of backlash for the decision that I had made. But I also know that, through sharing my story, I can also help so many others through their experiences and help others come to a decision that is only right for them. To terminate or not to terminate, that is a decision only the bearer can make and should have the freedom to do so without judgement. And this is why I am writing this book. Not to take on the negativity from those with opposing beliefs, but to help those who need a hand with their own decisions, and their own guidance and healing during a similar experience. So that they know they are not alone and that we will stand together and support one another as human kind should.

CHAPTER 17

Healing

Even though my friends support was much appreciated and I will always be grateful for it, I realized that it just wasn't enough at the time. So I reached out for counselling. I was aware that I was having feelings and emotions that I have never felt before, and I had no idea of how to cope. I never actually followed through, however, with the counselling sessions. And the reasons will be discussed in a later chapter of this book. I do recommend to anyone who feels they need extra support, to seek the help that they need. Situations like these are much too difficult to experience all alone. If counselling is not an option at the time, perhaps there is a trusted friend or family member that can support you through the process. No one should ever have to bear this weight alone. There are support centres and help lines that are available to anyone in need. Find what is available in your area and please don't hesitate to reach out.

If I would have followed through with the counselling sessions, I do believe that the recovery process would have went much smoother. I do believe that openly discussing such situations is extremely beneficial for mental and physical health.

My entire world evolved around the termination at this time. It was all I could think about. I felt sadness, grief, anger and resentment. And it was about 2 months post termination that I really began to do some growth and development and self-wellness work. And I was introduced to a whole new world. A world that I knew existed, but one that I never actively paid attention to or participated much in. I began reading all the time and constantly learning and growing as a person.

It wasn't too long post termination that I found a community of individuals who are likeminded and strive for the same goals in life as I do. Goals to create a happier and more fulfilling life. Goals to create success for ourselves. I think that the timing of this community couldn't be any more perfect. There is one saying that someone had mentioned along the way and it really had an impact on my perspective of the world. The saying was "the universe is constantly working towards equilibrium to balance itself out. So when something bad happens, something equally as good, or better, has to happen to equal out". This statement alone has gotten me through tough moments and allowed me to look towards the future with hope and faith. And I believe that I was guided to this community, not forget about the bad, but to bring the good so that I could heal.

Even though this community had no idea what I had been through, because I never told any of them, it was through this community that my healing really began to really take place. I was constantly working on my wellness through reading self-growth and development books and working through wellness workbooks. And through the healing process, I became aware that everything that happens in our lives, just happens. And it is our perspectives, which are built from our most inner core beliefs, which shape those perspectives. So we can view a circumstance or situation to be good or bad, and that may be our truth. But it doesn't necessarily mean that it is either good or bad, it is simply how we perceive it to be. And I had come to my own realization that what had happened in my life, wasn't either good or bad, it just was. And I had the power to put whatever label onto it that I wanted. And this knowledge is a very powerful thing. It was my first major step towards healing.

There are so many ways that a person can embrace the healing process. Writing was also a huge healing piece for me. Writing my story and getting it out there has really helped with processing the thoughts that went along with what I perceived as a traumatic experience. Talking with friends and family helped too because it helped me to realize that there are many other people who share the same beliefs that I do and it definitely helped me to cope.

Of course healing didn't magically happen over-night. There are times that I still feel intense grief. Not to the point that it is paralyzing, but enough to change my mood in a negative manner. Music seems to have the most effect when it comes to grief stricken flashbacks. There are those moments when I will be walking in a grocery store and 'our' song would come on and it would feel as though a shock would be sent straight through my body. I instantly feel overwhelmed with sadness. Sadness over the entire traumatic experience and sadness over the love that I once had but lost, sadness over what could have been, sadness about having to make that big decision. Sometimes when I know that there is a song that triggers negative memories I will play it over and over again. This helps me to bring forward the emotions I am having, accept them for what they are, and to work through them. If I do this long enough then I am able to associate different emotions with the songs and then when these songs come on the radio when I am not expecting it then it doesn't have such a negative impact on my mood.

It takes time to heal and maybe in some circumstances we might never be completely healed from a situation. However, it is possible to make sense of and overcome traumatic obstacles with help so don't be afraid to ask for help or guidance from people or sources that you trust. Remember that it is important to be patient with the healing process because we all heal so differently.

I talk a lot about having support. But that wasn't always the case. There were so many times and days that I felt very alone. Times when I really needed someone, there wasn't anyone there for me. Not because they didn't care. But perhaps because I did not know how to ask for support or maybe I didn't know exactly what kind of support I needed. Sometimes I felt so incredibly alone. I remember that on the day that the termination took place, I asked a couple people to watch my boys. I wasn't overly persistent but I also wasn't comfortable with them there with me while this took place. I shielded them from the whole experience and they do not know what happened and I don't plan to tell them until they are much older, if ever. But they were in the next room while the termination was taking place because I didn't get anyone to watch them. And of course with that came another layer of guilt. I didn't always have someone I could rely on. All of those days I spent crying. I was alone. I am aware this this may be the case for many people. It isn't that the support isn't there. But it is incredibly difficult to reach out as well. I just want assure you that if you are feeling alone, you are not. We are in this together. And you are so strong for being able to get through this difficult time. And you will get through it. Trust yourself, only you know what's best for you.

Printed in the United States
by Baker & Taylor Publisher Services